# BRITISH
# WILD
# ANIMALS

Glenetive Primary School.

Session 1981-82.

Presented

to

Louise Hunter

for

Perfect Attendance

in

Class I.

# BRITISH WILD ANIMALS

WILD MAMMALS OF THE BRITISH ISLES

Photographs by
**GEOFFREY KINNS**

Devised and Written by
**BRIAN GRIMES**

BOOK CLUB ASSOCIATES
LONDON

This edition published 1981 by
Book Club Associates by
arrangement with Hodder and Stoughton
Children's Books, a division of Hodder and
Stoughton Ltd, Mill Road, Dunton Green,
Sevenoaks, Kent TN13 2YJ.

Printed in Italy.

Photoset by Rowland Phototypesetting
Limited, Bury St Edmunds, Suffolk.
Origination by Anglia Reproductions Limited,
Witham, Essex.

# INTRODUCTION

The species of mammals in the British Isles evolved as a result of at least six waves of invaders associated with the last Ice Age and the following alternating periods of warm and cold conditions. It seems unlikely, however, that many species survived that series of changing events. As the final wave of invading mammals, in the warmer climate of the Post-Glacial times, advanced northwards, some were unable to reach Ireland or many of the smaller islands which had now become separated from the 'mainland' of Britain. Ultimately, the British Isles were detached from the continent of Europe by the waters of the North Sea and the English Channel, instead of the easily crossed fens and swamps which had previously been there.

Our mammals, then, have been isolated from the main stocks of European mammals for only about 7,000 years. This period is apparently not sufficient for the development of distinct species. However, some that have been separated from their continental relations for that period have become slightly different and are now considered to be distinct sub-species.

The important characteristics of mammals are their ability to produce milk to suckle their young from the mammary glands; to give birth to live young; and to grow hair – even the hedgehog's spines are modified hairs. They are warm blooded, and with a high degree of intelligence. It is this intelligence that has helped mammals to adjust successfully, when changes in conditions have required some alterations in their behavioural patterns.

In the British Isles, wild animals are not so easily seen in the landscape as birds are, although the rabbit, deer and squirrel are exceptions, but it is difficult to see even these species at close quarters. Many are nocturnal in their habits, and others are specialists in the art of concealment. Although so rarely seen, mammals are very numerous: the population of field mice probably exceeds that of man.

The more recent invaders to our shores have in most instances been unwelcome. Species such as the grey squirrel, coypu, muskrat and mink frequently intrude on the habitats of the more integrated native mammals, and without the predators that would normally keep down their numbers, they can reproduce so that their populations may reach pest proportions. For example, the muskrat was introduced because of its fur, called 'musquash', and it became a pest after colonies developed from animals that had escaped from farms. They caused considerable damage to river banks and the surrounding farm land, but intensive trapping eliminated them in 1931. The greatest threat these aliens present to the indigenous mammals is in competition for food and habitats.

Some mammals disappeared from the British scene many years ago: the bear was probably exterminated by the end of the 10th century, although the animals were imported for bear-baiting until the 19th century. The wolf finally disappeared in the 18th century, after years of persecution had driven it to the north of Scotland. Indeed, our carnivores have been persecuted throughout the ages, although there has recently been a greater appreciation of the importance of the role they play in the so called 'balance of nature' of the countryside.

The larger carnivores remaining in these islands, the fox, badger, otter, polecat, wild cat and pine marten, have been able to survive for various reasons. The polecat, marten and wild cat are restricted to the remoter parts of Scotland and Wales. The current development of the forests and the establishment of Nature Reserves in these areas should ensure a future for these species. The fox is numerous because it is often preserved for hunting, and it has, in recent years, adapted to life in urban areas. The badger is inoffensive, and has few natural enemies apart from man. The Badger Act of 1973 made it illegal to kill badgers without authority, or to keep them as pets, so their future seems secure. Recently, however, bovine tuberculosis in badgers has been found in the south-west of England. Accumulated evidence seems to confirm that infected badgers transmit the disease to cattle, and such badgers have had to be gassed.

The otter occurs throughout the British Isles, and is now a protected species. There is serious concern for its future, however, as a result of the decrease of water habitats and the probable injurious effects of polluted rivers and streams, which are particularly harmful to young otters. Research is necessary to obtain realistic figures for the total population distribution, and the causes of decline in this animal, so that action can be taken to ensure its future. There have been recent reports of otters being trapped and drowned in lobster pots in Scottish sea lochs.

The stoat and weasel are more widespread than the large carnivores. Although many regard them as vermin, because they kill game birds and poultry, it is now recognised that this habit is compensated by their valuable role in destroying pests such as rabbits, voles, mice and rats.

Probably no other country of comparable size has such a range of

Otter

environmental conditions as the British Isles, with the contrasts provided by the highlands of the north and west and the drier lowlands of the south and east. Within this small area exists a wide variety of habitats. These islands are very crowded, and there are considerable and conflicting claims for our limited resources. Many of these interests are incompatible with those of conservation of wildlife. The greatest threat to our mammals is the destruction and the deterioration of habitats because of the demands for industrial development, more intensive farming practices, the effects of pollution, and the increasing calls on the countryside for leisure and recreation facilities. But not all change is detrimental to wildlife – old gravel pits and reservoirs are examples of helpful changes. It is also possible that some types of recreation and leisure activities can be compatible with nature conservation and forestry.

A newly-born Fallow fawn, only fifteen minutes old

Wherever possible, a planned multiple-use of the land should be encouraged and developed. Such an approach offers the most effective means of conserving our wildlife.

Through the media of books, radio and television, a greater knowledge of our mammals is becoming widespread throughout the country. This knowledge should stimulate people's interest in the welfare of mammals, as is evident from the growing support of voluntary organisations concerned with conservation. Even so, we must not become complacent, because the destruction of habitats is a continuing process, and we must always be alert to ensure that important sites are safeguarded. The intention of this book is to bring to the home pictures of the interesting and elusive British mammals. It is hoped that they will further arouse appreciation and awareness, and consequently a deeper sympathy with our fifty or so land mammals and two resident seals.

# GROUPS OF BRITISH MAMMALS

| Order | English name | Family name |
|---|---|---|
| *MARSUPIALIA* | **Red-necked wallabies** | *Macropodidae* |
| *INSECTIVORA* | **Hedgehogs** | *Erinaceidae* |
| | **Moles** | *Talpidae* |
| | **Shrews** | *Soricidae* |
| *CHIROPTERA* | **Bats** | |
| | **Horseshoe** | *Rhinolophidae* |
| | **Whiskered** | *Vespertilionidae* |
| | **Natterer's** | *Vespertilionidae* |
| | **Daubenton's** | *Vespertilionidae* |
| | **Serotine** | *Vespertilionidae* |
| | **Leisler's** | *Vespertilionidae* |
| | **Noctule** | *Vespertilionidae* |
| | **Pipestrelle** | *Vespertilionidae* |
| | **Common Long-eared** | *Vespertilionidae* |

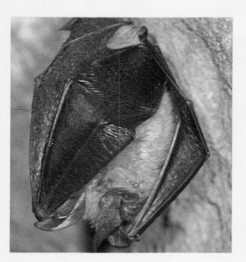

| | | |
|---|---|---|
| *LAGOMORPHA* | **Rabbits and Hares** | *Leporidae* |
| | | |
| *RODENTIA* | **Squirrels** | *Scuiridae* |
| | **Voles** | *Cricetidae/ Microtinae* |
| | **Mice and Rats** | *Muridae* |
| | **Dormice** | *Gliridae* |
| | **Coypu** | *Capromyidae* |
| | | |
| *CARNIVORA* | **Foxes** | *Canidae* |
| | **Pine martens** | *Mustelidae* |
| | **Weasels** | *Mustelidae* |
| | **Stoats** | *Mustelidae* |
| | **Polecats** | *Mustelidae* |
| | **Mink** | *Mustelidae* |
| | **Badgers** | *Mustelidae* |
| | **Otters** | *Mustelidae* |
| | **Wild cats** | *Felidae* |
| | | |
| *PINNIPEDIA* | **Seals** | *Phocidae* |
| | | |
| *PERISSODACTYLA* | **Horses** | *Equidae* |
| | | |
| *ARTIODACTYLA* | **Deer** | *Cervidae* |
| | **Goats** | *Bovidae* |
| | **Sheep** | *Bovidae* |

# MARSUPIALS

*MARSUPIALIA*

These are members of the order of pouched mammals. The young marsupial is not fully developed at birth and seeks the safety of its mother's pouch, where it is suckled until it has completed its development. A kangaroo's pouch is so placed because it spends much of its life in an upright position, but the bandicoot has a pouch between its hind legs, because it runs on all fours. Apart from the oppossum of North America, all marsupials are found in Australasia.

# RED-NECKED or Bennett's Wallaby

*Wallabia rufoguscus*

This is the one species living in a feral state in Britain. A Tasmanian sub-species was established in the Peak District at a small zoo in the mid-1930s, from whence the animals escaped, during the 1939–45 war. This colony suffered badly during the severe winter of 1978–9, and their estimated population in 1980 was only 12. The diet of these wallabies consists mainly of heather, bilberries, leaves and grasses. There is also a colony in the Sussex Weald, which lives in a more wooded environment. Red-necked wallabies were introduced at Leonardslee Park, Sussex, but some escaped and a small feral population established itself. Although no figures are available regarding the total Sussex population, several sightings have been recorded recently in the East Grinstead, Crawley and Cuckfield areas. The average length of head and body is 65cm, and the tail is almost as long – an additional 62cm.

# HEDGEHOGS, MOLES AND SHREWS

## INSECTIVORA

There are more than 270 species of this order in the world. The British insect-eating mammals, excluding the hedgehogs, are very small. Although the name suggests an exclusive diet of insects, they do occasionally eat vegetative matter. Hedgehogs have a great liking for bread and milk. Moles and shrews are voracious eaters, and their life is an unceasing search for food, as they must consume more than their own body weight every 24 hours. The subterranean habits of the mole and the burrowing of the shrews make tracking difficult.

Hedgehogs and water shrews are more easily tracked because of their size, and, in the case of the latter, because the animal prefers waterside habitats.

## HEDGEHOG

*Erinaceus europaeus*

These familiar, short-legged animals are found in most parts of the British Isles. They are abundant in grassland, deciduous woodlands and hedgerows, and have become common in suburban areas. This incursion into suburbia is evident from the numbers of dead hedgehogs found on the roads. Like most insect-eating animals, they have poor sight, and can easily be caught. They are very verminous being infected by fleas, and sometimes lice as well. Usually hibernation begins about October and ends in April. The average length of male head and body is 26cm.

Left: A family of young Hedgehogs

# COMMON MOLE

*Talpa europaea*

Moles are efficient burrowing machines. Their forefeet are used to excavate the tunnels where they spend almost their entire lives. Food consists of insects, worms and slugs. Their presence is reliably indicated by the large mounds they leave behind after their tunnelling activities. Larger mounds, called 'fortresses' and containing a nest chamber, become covered with grasses, weeds, and on chalk grasslands with wild thyme. The average length of head and body is 12–15cm.

# PYGMY SHREW

*Sorex minutus*

One of the smallest British mammals, head and body measuring only 4–6cm, it is found throughout the British Isles, except the Shetlands, Scilly, and Channel Islands. These animals do not make their own burrows, but use those made by others. Their diet consists mainly of spiders and beetles, and they are active during both day and night.

Below: Common Mole
Right: Pygmy Shrew

## COMMON SHREW

*Sorex araneus*

This species is common throughout England, Scotland and Wales, but is absent from the Isle of Man, the Outer Hebrides, the Northern Isles, and from Ireland. They use old mice runs, but will tunnel their own burrows in leaf litter and soil. They are solitary animals, and can be very aggressive. They are found in grassland, hedgerows, woodlands and grassy banks. Their diet is similar to that of the pygmy shrew, consisting of spiders, earthworms and insects. The average length of head and body is 6–8cm.

## WATER SHREW

*Neomys fodiens*

Water shrews are found throughout Britain, but like the common shrew, the species is absent from Ireland. As the name implies, they are located on or near water. Extensive shallow burrows are tunnelled in banks, with the entrance either above or below the water. They are larger than common shrews, with an average length of head and body of 9cm.

Above: Common Shrew
Right: Water Shrew

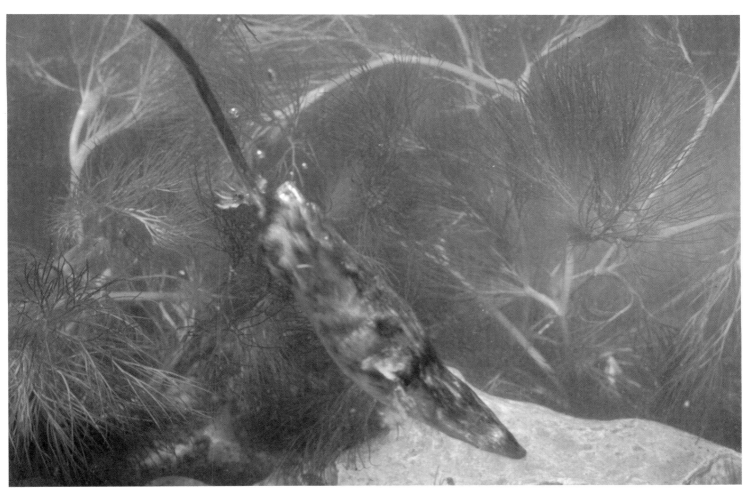

# LESSER WHITE-TOOTHED SHREW or Isles of Scilly Shrew

*Crocidura suaveolens*

This species is only found on the Isles of Scilly and the Channel Islands. They can be distinguished from their mainland relative, the common shrew, by their more prominent ears. They are generally found in vegetation and along the rocky shores. The length of head and body is 5.5–7.5cm.

# BATS

*CHIROPTERA*

Although some people are strangely prejudiced against bats, they are interesting and useful mammals, and theirs is one of the largest orders – about 900 species are known throughout the world, and the British Isles have 15 resident species. Bats are the only mammals that have achieved true flight, although some other mammals are able to glide. They can be separated into two groups: the fruit-eaters and the insect-eaters. The British species belong to the latter category, and they hunt and eat on the wing. Insect-eating bats are smaller than the fruit-eaters. They have poor eyesight, but have developed a highly efficient system of echo-location, which enables them to catch insects and to avoid obstructions during their flights.

Pipestrelle Bat and young

# GREATER HORSESHOE BAT

*Rhinolophus ferrumequinum*

These large bats have a wing span of about 37cm, and are confined to south-west England and parts of South Wales. They hibernate in caves, but in the summer months prefer roofs and barns. They feed mainly on flying insects.

# LESSER HORSESHOE BAT

*Rhinolophus hipposideros*

These bats look very similar to the greater horseshoe bats, but are smaller, with a wing span of only 23cm. They are found more extensively, in almost the whole of Wales, south-west England and Galway, Western Ireland. They feed on beetles, spiders and moths.

Above top: The Greater Horseshoe Bat displays the lobes of bare skin on its muzzle from which it gets its name
Left: A Greater and two Lesser Horseshoe Bats roost together

# WHISKERED BAT

*Myotis mystacinus*

Records are limited, but this species is probably common throughout England and Wales, but not Scotland. These are small bats, with a wing span of 22cm. They prefer open country and woodlands. During the summer they roost in buildings and trees, and are often seen before sunset. The diet consists essentially of flies, beetles, spiders and moths.

# NATTERER'S BAT

*Myotis nattereri*

They are distributed throughout the British Isles, apart from the northern counties of Scotland, and are medium sized bats, with a wing span of 27cm. They emerge from their roosts after sunset, these roosts usually being in hollow trees or old buildings. Their diet consists of flies, moths and beetles. As well as catching insects in flight, they will also take food off foliage.

Far left: Whiskered Bat
Left: Natterer's Bat

29

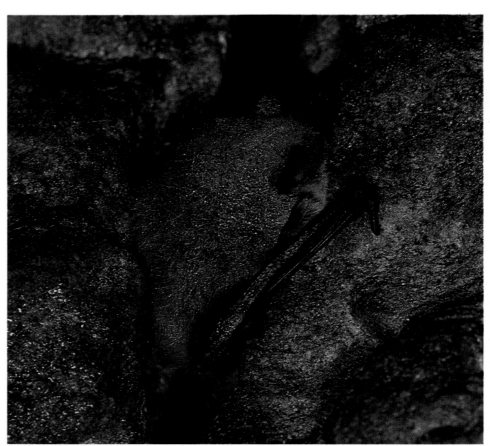

Right: A frost covered Daubenton's Bat
hibernates in a crevice
Below: Daubenton's Bat feeding

# DAUBENTON'S BAT

*Myotis daubentoni*

These bats are found througout the British Isles, except for the extreme northern counties of Scotland. Occasionally they are seen flying over water, as they appear to have a preference for woodland close to water. They eat mostly insects, which they catch during flights over water. They have a wing span of 24cm.

# SEROTINE BAT

*Eptesicus serotinus*

Their distribution in the British Isles is confined to East Anglia and southern England. They live in small colonies, and have a preference for holes in trees, but sometimes they use old buildings for roosting. They have a wing span of 36cm, and feed on insects and beetles.

Below: Serotine Bat

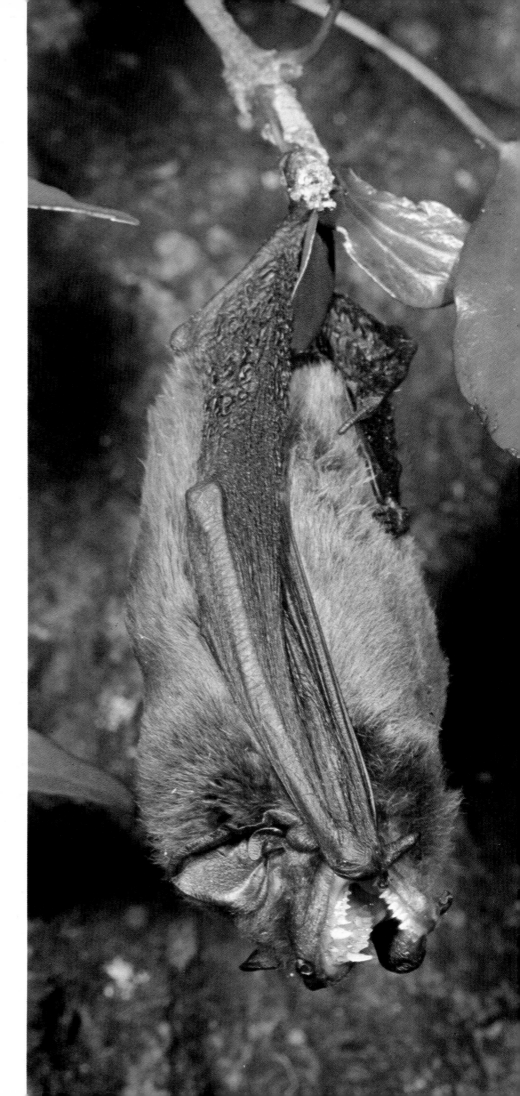

# LEISLER'S BAT

*Nyctalus leisleri*

They are distributed widely
throughout Ireland, but are found
only in the Midlands and southern
counties of England. They are
woodland bats, and live in colonies in
holes in trees, and sometimes in
buildings. Their wing span is 32cm,
and their food consists of insects
caught and eaten on the wing.

# NOCTULE BAT

*Nyctalus noctula*

This species is found throughout
England and Wales, but is rare in
Scotland and unknown in Ireland.
These are some of Britain's largest
bats, with a wing span of 35cm. They
usually roost in holes in trees, and
feed on insects which they catch and
eat during flight.

Right: Leisler's Bat yawning
Far right: Noctule Bat

32

# PIPESTRELLE BAT

*Pipistrellus pipistrellus*

These bats are common throughout
the British Isles, including most of
the larger islands. They live in
colonies, frequently near water, and
roost in trees, roofs, and buildings,
but are rarely to be found in caves.
Their food consists mainly of small
insects caught and eaten during
flight. Larger insects are usually
taken to a perch to be eaten. They
have a wing span of 22cm.

Left: Pipestrelle Bat
Above: Common Long Eared Bat

# COMMON LONG-EARED BAT

*Plecotus auritus*

As their name implies, their ears are
extremely long, which makes
identification easy. They are
distributed widely throughout the
British Isles, except for the northern
counties of Scotland. They are found
in large colonies, and roost under
roofs and in trees, hibernating in
caves during the winter. They have a
wing span of between 23–28cm.

# RABBITS AND HARES

*LAGOMORPHA*

Rabbits and hares were formerly classified as rodents, but although they have some similarities, detailed analysis has proved that they are not so closely related as to be included in the same order. They are now classified in this order.

Rabbits and hares are to be found in almost all parts of the world. There are only three species in the British Isles, the rabbit, the common hare and the mountain hare. They are herbivores, and prefer open country, with cover readily accessible. However, the mountain hare, as its name implies, favours the higher ground of Scotland and Ireland.

## RABBIT

*Oryctolagus cuniculus*

Rabbits were probably introduced to the British Isles during the 12th century, possibly from Spain, for their fur and meat. They were kept in warrens, and it is likely that the present day rabbit is a descendant of escapes from these. Rabbits are the victims of a number of predators, including the fox, wild cat, stoat and weasel, but their reproductive capacity is so prolific that, given suitable conditions, they will rapidly achieve pest proportions. Myxomatosis has greatly reduced the density of rabbits in our countryside, but there is evidence that they are recovering, and in some areas have already regained their former numbers. They feed on a wide range of vegetation. The average length of head and body is 40cm.

# BROWN HARE

*Lepus capensis*

These are native to Britain and are found in lowland areas. They are not native to Ireland, and although attempts have been made to establish the breed there, it has not spread. Usually solitary, they prefer rough grassland areas. They do damage to crops and to some varieties of young trees, but do not pose so serious a problem to farmers as the rabbit. The average length of head and body is 55cm.

Right: Brown Hare
Far right above: Leverets
and far right below: Blue Hare

# BLUE HARE
## or Mountain Hare

*Lepus timidus*

This species of hare is confined to the Scottish Highlands, the Peak District, where it was introduced towards the end of the 19th century, and the whole of Ireland. Smaller than the brown hare, and with shorter ears, they feed on moorland vegetation, including heather and cotton grass. During the winter their coats may turn white, but occasionally will retain dark patches. The average length of head and body is 50cm.

# RODENTS

*RODENTIA*

Rodents are the most successful species of mammal. They are found in almost all environments of the world – deserts, mountains, tundra, built-up areas included. There are about 1600 species in the world, and there are probably a few species not yet recorded. There are only 15 species in the British Isles, and several of these have been introduced. Most rodents are small and defenceless, and form a major source of food for predators. However, because of their considerable reproductive capacity, their numbers are maintained.

Occasionally, some species reach plague proportions, and during these periods there may be large increases in the numbers of predatory birds. Owls consume large quantities of voles, mice, rats, moles and shrews. Rodents, whose teeth are developed for grinding, live mainly on vegetative matter, although some are insect-eaters, and others will eat anything that is available.

Most rodents are regarded as pests because of the considerable damage that they may cause to seedlings in forests, to food stocks in warehouses, and to growing crops. Rats are notorious because of their connection with the spread of bubonic plague which was transmitted by the rat flea.

Field Vole and young in their nest

# RED SQUIRREL

*Sciurus vulgaris*

These native squirrels with their prominent ear tufts and reddish grey colouring were once widely distributed throughout the British Isles. The population has fluctuated; the present decline is due to loss of habitat, and then occupation by the grey squirrel may prevent recolonisation. Red squirrels are still abundant in Scotland, parts of Wales, East Anglia, Ireland and the Isle of Wight. They are seen in large numbers in conifer woodlands, which supply the squirrels' food and cover. Their diet consists of nuts, pine seeds, acorns, beech mast and some fungi. A large nest, called a 'drey', is loosely constructed of twigs, bark and leaves. The average length of head and body is 22cm, and the tail length is 17–20cm.

42

44

# GREY SQUIRREL

*Sciurus carolinensis*

These familiar animals are now widespread throughout England and Wales, and lowland Scotland. In Ireland they are confined to the central counties. They were introduced from America at the end of the last century, when a colony was started at Woburn, Bedfordshire. They are distinguished from the red squirrel by their larger size, lack of ear tufts and colour. Their food consists of fir cone seeds, the fruits of most trees, nuts, grain, and sometimes eggs and young birds. The average length of head and body is 28cm, and the tail about 21cm.

Below: A typical squirrel's drey

## BANK VOLE

*Clethrionomys glareolus*

They are distributed throughout England, Scotland and Wales, but in Ireland are confined to a small area in the south-west. They are active by both day and night, prefer woodlands, hedgerows and banks covered with rough grass and make extensive runs in ground vegetation. The average length of head and body is 9cm.

## FIELD VOLE

*Microtus agrestis*

Field voles are widespread throughout England, Scotland and Wales, but are absent from Ireland. They prefer rough grassland, and make networks of tunnels. Under favourable conditions they may reach plague proportions and cause damage to vegetation and to young plantations. These animals are active during both day and night. The average length of head and body is 10cm.

Above: Bank Vole and right: Field Vole

Left: A typical vole s nest

# WATER VOLE

*Arvicola terrestris*

These are found throughout Britain but not in Ireland. They are active during the day, and will sometimes store food below ground. Their diet consists principally of vegetative matter, although they occasionally eat fish. These voles are usually found along banks of rivers, streams, ditches and canals, and are often mistakenly called water 'rats'. The average length of head and body is 19cm.

Signs of a Water Vole, top: A Swimway, below: Holes in the river bank

Left: Wood mouse and young
Top right: Wood mice quarrelling

# WOOD MOUSE
## or Long-Tailed Field Mouse

*Apodemus sylvaticus*

They are distributed throughout the British Isles. They are active mainly at night, and they construct a network of tunnels. As their name implies, the most favoured habitat is woodland, but they are also found in gardens, hedgerows and pasture land. Their diet consists of fruits, slugs, snails and seedlings. The average length of head and body is 9cm.

# HARVEST MOUSE

*Micromys minutus*

Their distribution is confined to an area south of the River Tees. They are the smallest of British rodents, weighing only 6gm, and measuring, head and body, only 6cm. Their habitats are usually areas of dense vegetation, in open countryside and hedgerows where they can find cover and food. The diet is one of seeds, berries and insects.

Left: Harvest Mouse and below: House Mouse

# HOUSE MOUSE

*Mus musculus*

They are widespread throughout the British Isles, and are found in a wide variety of habitats, including fields, hedgerows and buildings. House mice can be harmful to man, as they carry many infectious diseases, and also cause much damage to food stores. The average length of head and body is 8cm.

54

# ST KILDA FIELD MOUSE

*Apodemus sylvaticus hirtensis*

This island variety is larger than its mainland relative, *Apodemus sylvaticus*. These mice are found on the main islands of the St Kilda group, and were probably introduced by the early settlers on Hirta, which was the only inhabited island of the group. The length of head and body is about 11cm.

# HEBRIDEAN FIELD MOUSE

*Apodemus sylvaticus hebridensis*

They are found on most of the Hebridean islands. Their colouring is very variable, and like the St Kilda field mouse they are larger than their mainland relative *Apodemus sylvaticus*. The length of head and body is 11cm.

# YELLOW-NECKED MOUSE

*Apodemus flavicollis*

These can be distinguished from the wood mouse, *Apodemus sylvaticus*, by their yellow collar and whitish under parts, and by the upper parts being reddish brown; also by their larger size. They are distributed throughout southern England and Wales, and occur in woodlands, hedgerows, and occasionally in gardens and houses. The length of body and head is 10–12cm.

Top left: St Kilda Field Mouse
Below left: Hebridean Field Mouse
Below right: Yellow-Necked Mouse

## BLACK RAT
## or Ship Rat

*Rattus rattus*

These rats originated in Asia, and are thought to have been brought to these shores from the Near East between the 10th and 11th centuries. They were once widespread over the whole of Britain, but are now confined to the larger port areas, and are almost exclusively nocturnal. The average length of head and body is 22cm, the tail being longer than the body.

Above: Black Rat and right: Brown Rat

## BROWN RAT
## or Norway Rat

*Rattus norvegicus*

These are widespread throughout the British Isles, and probably arrived here during the 18th century, after journeying to northern Europe, possibly from Central Asia. Brown rats are very aggressive, and the conflict which ensued between them and black rats almost reduced the latter to extinction. They can cause extensive damage to food stores in warehouses, and are capable of gnawing through thick wood and wire mesh. They construct complicated tunnel systems, and are also associated with sewers and refuse tips. The average length of head and body is 28cm.

Right: Common Dormouse hibernating
Below: Common Dormouse and nest

# COMMON DORMOUSE

*Muscardinus avellanarius*

They occur mainly in the south of England, with small populations in the Midlands and Wales, but are absent from Scotland and Ireland. They are agile climbers and can swim. They hibernate during the winter months, and prefer established deciduous woodland with a shrub layer and an ample supply of fruit, beech mast, hazel nuts and chestnuts. The average length of head and body is 8cm.

# FAT DORMOUSE

*Glis glis*

They are sometimes known as the 'edible dormouse'. They were introduced to England at the beginning of this century, to Hertfordshire, but their spread has been very limited. The fat dormouse favours woodlands and gardens, and is nocturnal. Their diet consists of fruit, nuts, and occasionally birds' eggs and insects. The average length of head and body is 15cm.

Above: Fat Dormouse

# COYPU

*Myocastor coypus*

These large animals are natives of South America, and were introduced to England for their fur. They have been very successful in colonising new habitats where conditions are favourable. Many escapes occurred during the last war, but only in the Fens and Norfolk did the coypu reach pest proportions. They are herbivorous, and cause considerable damage to crops and to dykes. The average length of head and body is 60cm.

# CARNIVORES

*CARNIVORA*

Carnivores are flesh-eating mammals that display a wide variety of forms, and have a high degree of intelligence. As a result of their continued persecution by man, most species conceal their activities; others, however, have been domesticated, such as the dog and the cat. Even foxes and badgers, if captured at a very early age, will adapt themselves to a life of domesticity, but the Scottish wild cat always remains untameable.

Scottish Wildcat

# FOX

*Vulpes vulpes*

Foxes are distributed throughout the British Isles, and although they are to be found on Skye, they are absent from some of the Scottish Isles. In areas where foxes are not preserved for hunting many efforts have been made to reduce their numbers, yet they remain abundant, and this demonstrates the tenacity and hardiness of the animals. They are mainly active between dusk and dawn, and eat, for the most part, voles, mice and rabbits. Foxes are untidy animals, and often leave the remains of food scattered outside their earths. They can also be detected by their strong, musky smell. The male is larger than the female, and the average length of head and body of the male is 66cm.

Above: A Fox cub emerges
from the earth

Above: Fox cubs, about six weeks old
Left: A newly dug earth

# PINE MARTEN

*Martes martes*

These were formerly widespread throughout the British Isles, but they are now restricted to the north-west of Scotland, and to a few isolated pockets in England and Wales. There is evidence that their numbers are increasing in Scotland, and this could be the result of the increasing acreage of conifer woodland. They are mainly nocturnal, spending much of their time in trees so that they are rarely seen. Their diet consists of small mammals and birds, and sometimes berries are eaten. The average length of head and body is 46cm. Their hunting territory may vary from 1–20 sq km.

Left: A typical Pine Marten's breeding area

# STOAT

*Mustela ermina*

They are distributed throughout the British Isles, with the exception of the Outer Hebrides and the Orkneys. They are distinguished from their close relative, the weasel, by their larger size and by the black tip to the tail. In Scotland the stoat develops a white coat during the winter months, but the tip of the tail remains black. The rabbit was the staple food of the stoat until myxomatosis occurred in 1954: now the stoat's food consists essentially of small mammals, and occasionally birds. The average length of head and body is 29cm.

# WEASEL

*Mustela nivalis*

They are common throughout Britain, but do not occur in Ireland or the outlying Scottish islands. They are found principally in areas where the undergrowth is dense and where rodents are plentiful. Small rodents are the weasel's main source of food. They are active both by day and night. The average length of head and body is 20cm.

# POLECAT

*Mustela putorius*

Polecats have been exterminated from England and Scotland, and do not occur in Ireland. However, they are found in Wales, where wooded hillsides, marshlands and bogs are frequented by these animals. They eat rodents, and occasionally birds, insects and amphibians. The average length of head and body is 41cm.

# MINK

*Mustela vison*

Mink were introduced to the British Isles from the USA for fur farming, in 1929; many escapes occurred, and wild colonies developed, especially in the south and south-west of England. Little information is available of their effects on British wildlife. They are mainly nocturnal, and are very good swimmers. Their diet consists of some birds, rats, voles, young rabbits and fish. The average head and body length is 35–45cm.

Left: Welsh Polecat/ferret variation and above: Mink

# BADGER

*Meles meles*

They are common throughout the British Isles, except for the Outer Isles of Scotland. Badgers are nocturnal, and live in setts tunnelled in well-drained soils, often under tree roots. They are largely omnivorous, eating small rodents, frogs, insects, molluscs and some vegetable matter. The average length of the male's head and body is 77cm, and they weigh about 12kg.

Badger cubs in their nests

Above: Three-month-old Badger cub
Right: A Badger at the entrance to a sett
with a pile of old bedding which has
been cleared out

# OTTER

*Lutra lutra*

These animals which were once common throughout the British Isles have recently suffered a severe decline in numbers due to loss of habitat through drainage, clearance and pollution. However, in Scotland they appear more plentiful. They are restless and playful creatures, and may wander extensively. Their diet consists of fish, occasional water birds and their young, small mammals and crustacea. The average length of head and body of a dog otter is 69cm., the female being smaller.

Carna Island, Argyllshire, home of Otters, Seals and Wildcats

Above: Otter tracks
Right centre: An Otter kill,
an eight-pound salmon

78

# WILD CAT

*Felis silvestris*

Although in appearance they are similar to the common alley tabby, the behaviour of wild cats is quite different. Even if raised from kittenhood by hand, they are never completely tamed, and will adopt a ferocious attitude towards strangers. They are confined mainly to north-western Scotland, preferring the rocky mountain-sides, grouse moors and forests, but they appear to be extending their range. Their food consists of rodents, usually voles, and occasionally of birds and fish. The average length of head and body is 60cm.

# SEALS

This order includes the walrus and the sealion, but only two species, the grey and the common seal are resident around the coasts of the British Isles. From time to time other wandering seals from the Arctic appear along our shores. Their main predator is man, and so the more inaccessible regions of the coast are chosen for their breeding grounds, called rookeries. When the pups are born and are still helpless, both they and their parents are vulnerable. The common seal prefers shallow sheltered waters, particularly mud and sandbanks. The grey seal favours the more rocky habitats, although it can also be found in estuaries, where, occasionally, both species occur together. Their graceful movements in the water are reduced to slow and clumsy movements on land.

Left: Common Seals
Below: A three day old Grey Seal pup

# COMMON SEAL

*Phoca vitulina*

Despite their English name, they are probably no more common than the grey seal. Common seals frequent the west coast of Scotland, and the east coast of England. They are also found along the west and south-east coasts of Ireland. They are rare along the coast of south and south-east England. They prefer shallow and well sheltered waters, sea lochs and estuaries, but occasionally rest on rocky ledges in northern Scotland. They eat all types of fish and molluscs. Their breeding grounds are known as rookeries, and the common seal pups are born with a grey coat, their white fur being moulted before birth. The average length of a male adult is 150cm, and of the female 140cm.

# GREY SEAL or Atlantic Seal

*Halichoerus grypus*

There are three distinct populations of this seal, those of the Baltic Sea, the Eastern Atlantic and the Western Atlantic. They differ in their breeding period, the Eastern Atlantic seals usually producing their young in the autumn, and the other two groups in spring and winter. The eastern Atlantic colonies form most of the British populations. These resident seals prefer rocky cliffs, caves and remote, uninhabited islands. Occasionally they are located on sandbanks. With the possible exceptions of the coasts of Kent and Sussex, they can be found along the whole of the coastline of the British Isles. They eat about 5–7kg of fish each day, except during breeding, when both sexes fast. The average length of the male adult is 205cm, and that of the female 180cm.

# HORSE

*PERISSODACTYLA*

Wild horses once abounded on the grassy plains of these islands, until about 10,000 years ago. The only true descendants of the wild horses which once roamed throughout Europe and Asia are now only to be found in Central Asia and Mongolia. The horse's hoof developed from a toe, and this enabled the animal to run fast over the grassy plains that existed in former times during the horse's development. There are a number of breeds living in a semi-wild state in the British Isles now, including the New Forest, Shetland, Welsh, Rhum and Exmoor ponies, and others. There are no truly wild horses.

## NEW FOREST PONY

*Equus caballus*

These very popular ponies are hardy and make very good mounts for children. Many different breeds have been introduced to the New Forest, and this cross breeding is responsible for the different types and the variety of colours. They are up to 14 hands high (a hand is 4 inches), 142cm at the shoulder.

## SHETLAND PONY

*Equus caballus*

These are the smallest working ponies in the British Isles, measuring only about 11 hands, 108cm, at the shoulder. Although they are so small they are very strong, and were used as work horses in the Shetlands and the Orkneys. It is possible that the modern Shetland pony is a descendant of the now extinct tarpan, which once roamed the steppes of Russia and Mongolia.

Far left: New Forest Pony and foal
Left: Shetland Pony

# DEER

*ARTIODACTYLA*

Only two of the deer family in the British Isles are truly native, the red and the roe deer. A further four species, the muntjac, sika deer, Chinese water deer, and the fallow deer are escapees from zoos or parks, or have been introduced by man. These have formed feral populations. The reindeer has been reintroduced to the Cairngorms in Scotland, but cannot be regarded as feral as it is a managed herd. The horns of the deer are solid; they are shed annually, and are borne by the males only, with the exception of the reindeer. The new growth is covered with a velvety skin which is cast off when it is fully grown, by scraping on trees.

Red Deer with her newly born calf in June

# RED DEER

*Cervus elaphus*

These are common in the north-west of Scotland, the western borders of Devon and Somerset, and they also occur in the New Forest. In Ireland they can be found in the south-west, the north-west, and in the east. During the spring they look very untidy, because they are shedding their winter coats, and the males are re-growing their antlers, which are still covered with the velvety skin.

Their food consists of young shoots from trees and shrubs, acorns, beech mast, chestnuts, berries, heather, lichens and tree bark. With the increased price of venison, attempts at farming deer are being made. The average stag has a head and body length of 183cm, the hind is smaller.

Above: Stags in velvet

Left: this stag has just
shed an antler
Below Left: Red Deer stag
Below: Hinds and calf at Torridon
in the Scottish Highlands

# SIKA DEER

*Cervus nippon*

These deer, which are common in Japan, are ideally suited to the cool, damp British climate. There are many established pockets of them in parts of the British Isles, including Hampshire, Yorkshire, Lancashire, Kintyre and Inverness-shire. They have a preference for deciduous woodland with dense undergrowth. They are most active at dusk and early morning, and are often seen grazing in fields close to woodlands. The average length of head and body is 140cm.

Right: Sika stag and hind sparring
Below: Young stag with developing antlers

Above: Sika stags in summer coats
Left: Winter colouring

Above: Fallow doe and calf
Right: Fallow buck in winter colouring

# FALLOW DEER

*Dama dama*

The most distinctive feature of the fallow bucks are the palmated (palm shaped) antlers. They are now distributed, if sparsely, throughout the British Isles, having been reintroduced to this country in about the 12th century. This species possibly became extinct during the end of the last inter-glacial period. They have a preference for lowland, deciduous woodland, with thick undergrowth. They feed on grasses, fresh tree foliage, fungi and fruit. The average length of head and body is 170cm.

Left: Buck and doe in October

# ROE DEER

*Capreolus capreolus*

These indigenous deer are widely distributed, though localised. They are common in Scotland, northern England, Hampshire and Dorset. During the winter months they congregate in small herds. They prefer conifer woodland with plenty of cover. They are active mainly at night, and their diet consists of leaves, berries, heather, clover and fungi. The average length of head and body is 115cm.

Far left: Doe, left: Buck and below: Fawn

# MUNTJAC

*Muntiacus reevesii*

Sometimes called the barking deer, the muntjac originated in China, and, as the result of escapes from parks at the beginning of this century, became established in the south-east of England. They prefer mixed or deciduous woodland with dense undergrowth. Their diet consists of young trees, fruits, berries, chestnuts and acorns. The average height at the shoulder is 52cm in the case of the male and 45cm, the female.

# CHINESE WATER DEER

*Hydropotes inermis*

These deer originated in China, and do not have any antlers. In England they have established themselves in the wild as a result of escapes from Woburn Park. Their habitat is usually grassy areas, and grass forms the main part of their diet, together with root crops. The average height at the shoulder of the male is 60cm, and of the female, 55cm.

Left: Muntjac and above: Chinese Water Deer

# REINDEER

*Rangifer tarandus*

Characteristic of the reindeer is the fact that both male and female have antlers. They were reintroduced, after possibly becoming extinct in this country during the last glacial period, to the Cairngorms in Scotland in the early 1950s, and have been reasonably successful as a managed herd. Their food consists of lichens, grasses, leaves and willow twigs. The average length of head and body is 200cm.

Left: Reindeer cow and calf
Below: Reindeer in winter colouring

# FERAL GOAT

*Capra hircus*

Wild goats are distributed in the
more remote parts of Scotland, Wales
and Ireland. They are capable of
digesting coarse vegetation, and so
thrive on areas avoided by sheep, and
are consequently found on rocky
hillsides. However, they will venture
to the outskirts of towns and villages
in the winter months in search of
food. Feral goats are descendants of
the domestic goat which was
imported from Asia. The average
male weighs between 25–45kg, and
the female between 25–35kg.

# FERAL SHEEP

*Ovis aries*

The only wild sheep in the British Isles are the Soay sheep on the island of Hirta in the St Kilda group, off the north-west coast of Scotland; those on Soay are not truly wild. The abandoned stone houses, called cleats, which were once used by the departed St Kildans to store food, are now used as shelter by the sheep in the winter months.

Feral Sheep, both the ram and ewe have horns

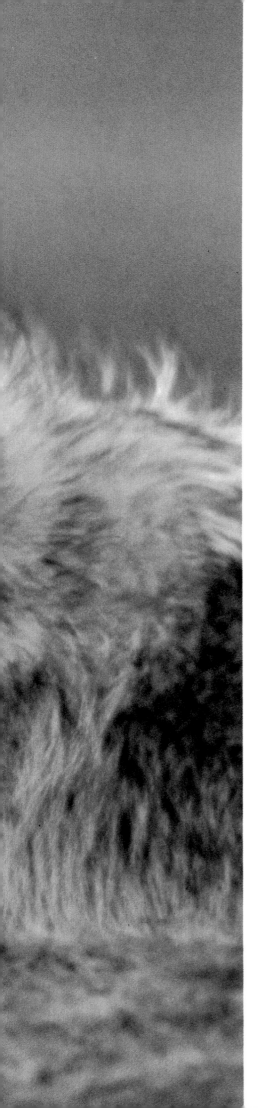

# PAST MAMMALS OF THE BRITISH ISLES

The only positive indication of the existence of prehistoric mammals in the British Isles is the presence of fossils in sedimentary rocks (limestone, sandstone and shales). The presence of fossils of animals found in a rock stratum denotes that such animals were alive at the time the rock was formed. Peat is also a preservative, and many animal remains have been found in peat bogs. One of the most interesting remains to have been found in peat in the British Isles was the antlers of an Irish Elk. This animal had enormous antlers that measured up to 427cm in length. Peat is a mass of plant remains, containing seeds and pollen; analysis has provided vital evidence in determining the evolution of British vegetation. These studies have proved valuable in identifying the periods of environmental changes in the vegetation, thus providing vital evidence of climatic changes, and changes in the types of animals. Deterioration of the climate was responsible for the extinction from these islands of the larger animals such as the elephant, the rhinoceros and the horse.

Many animals have died out in historic times, including the musk ox, the bear, the wolf and the elk, which survive in other parts of the world.

Wolf, extinct in Britain since the 18th century

# GROUPS OF PAST BRITISH MAMMALS

| Order | English name | Family name |
|---|---|---|
| *RODENTIA* | **European Beavers** | *Castoridae* |
| *CARNIVORA* | **Wolves** | *Canidae* |
| | **Northern Lynx** | *Felidae* |
| | **Brown Bears** | *Ursidae* |
| *PERISSODACTYLA* | **Wild Horses** | *Equidae* |
| *ARTIODACTYLA* | **Wild Boars** | *Suidae* |
| | **Elks or Moose** | *Cervidae* |
| | **European Bison** | *Bovidae* |
| | **Musk oxen** | *Bovidae* |

# BEAVER

*Castor fiber*

These are ideally adapted for an aquatic life, with their webbed hind feet and a paddle-like tail which is used as a rudder. They have survived in many parts of Europe, Asia and North America. They probably became extinct in the British Isles in about the 12th century, and their decline has been attributed to their being hunted by man. However, they are now protected, and are being reintroduced into their former habitats in parts of Europe. They live in 'lodges' and build large and elaborate dams. Average size 80–100cm.

# WOLF

*Canis lupus*

Wolves were once distributed throughout Europe, northern Asia and North America, but today they are confined to the more remote mountainous and wooded regions, where they live in families and hunt in packs. They are tireless hunters and usually catch their prey by attacking on the run. Wolves have been the subject of many imaginative bloodthirsty stories of attacks on man; such stories are probably without foundation. They are considered to be the ancestors of the domestic dog. Length of body is 100–150cm.

Below: A European Wolf bitch
Below right: A Lynx and her kitten

# NORTHERN LYNX

*Felis lynx*

Originally distributed over all parts of Europe but, due to the loss of habitat and hunting, they are now mainly confined to Scandinavia and the Carpathian mountains. There they inhabit the more densely wooded areas, where they use their agility and tree climbing ability to attack their prey. There is a southern variety of these mammals called the Pardel or Spanish Lynx, *Felis lynx pardina*, which as the name implies are native to Spain and they are also found in Portugal. Their diet consists mainly of small mammals, but they will attack young and weak deer. Length of body is 85–130cm.

# BROWN BEAR

*Ursus arctos*

Brown bears became extinct in the British Isles about the 10th century, but still survive in parts of Eastern Europe, Asia and North America. These animals were hunted for food, fur and for sport. They can measure up to 2 metres, and weigh about 300kg.

# HORSE

*Equus przewalskii*

These are the only truly wild horses to survive today, although many specimens have adapted successfully to a life in zoological gardens and parks. They usually live in small herds in semi-desert areas of eastern Asia. Shoulder height about 13 hands, 132cm.

Left: Brown Bear and cubs and above: Przewalskii's Wild Horse

# WILD BOAR

*Sus scrofa*

In former times wild boar were common in woodlands in the British Isles. They disappeared from these islands in the 17th century, but are still to be found in continental Europe and Asia. They are omnivorous, eating fruit, nuts and small vertebrates. The wild boar has developed large, protruding teeth which can inflict considerable damage on a would-be attacker. Length of body 110–130cm.

# ELK or Moose

*Alces alces*

These are the largest members of the deer family, and old males can weigh up to 800kg, but normally the average weight is 500kg. They are found mostly on the sub-arctic tundras of Alaska and Canada, where they feed on trees and aquatic vegetation. Recent conservation measures have resulted in the spread of this mammal in Europe, including Norway, Sweden, USSR, and other parts of north-western Europe. Fossil remains have been found in Norfolk. Length of body 250–270cm.

Above: Wild Boar
Right: Young bull Elk with developing antlers

# EUROPEAN BISON

*Bison bonasus*

These animals were widespread throughout the forests of Europe in historic times. Now, as a result of the destruction of forests, and because they have been hunted for food and clothing, they have become confined to an area along the Polish/Russian border, and in small herds in the region of the Caucasus mountains. The presence of the remains of these animals in Britain indicates a period of relatively warmer climate than existed during the times of the musk ox and elk. They measure 300–350cm in length.

Above right: European Bison bull and cow
Right: Bison cow. Both male and female have horns

# MUSK OX

*Ovibos moschatus*

Now inhabitants of the sub-Arctic regions of Alaska, Canada and Greenland, musk oxen have been reintroduced to Scandinavia. They live in herds, and when attacked, they form a defensive ring. The discovery of this animal's remains in the British Isles, as well as those of the elk, is evidence of the varying climatic conditions that existed here in prehistoric times. Length of body 190–240cm.

# THE PHOTOGRAPHER

*Since the last war Geoffrey Kinns has followed in the footsteps of the eminent pioneer photographer/naturalists, such as the Kearton brothers, R. B. Lodge, Oliver Pike and others, who at the beginning of this century were dedicated to the task of producing high quality photography so that the public should gain a better knowledge of Britain's wildlife. Geoffrey's name is always associated with his many masterpieces and his work is used for book illustration throughout the world. However, this is the first time that a book has been devoted entirely to his work.*

Geoffrey is a good example of 'hunter turned conservationist'. He was born in the foothills of the Himalayas at Naini Tal in India, the younger son of Hertfordshire parents. His father founded the Institute of Carpentry and Wood Technology at Barielly, Northern Central Province, India and was also an acting Major in the Indian Defence Force. Major Kinns killed and skinned over two thousand crocodiles in the Ganges, Rurgurga and other rivers near Bareilly, shooting crocodiles being essential to protect the Indian women and children who daily used the rivers for washing their clothes and bathing. Geoffrey accompanied his parents on several of these expeditions, and his father taught him how to stalk game and use an air rifle. Their happiest and most interesting times were spent at waterholes watching big game which included sambur, chital, wild boar and monkeys coming to drink. Young Geoffrey also liked to spend his time modelling animals in plasticine and playing with his various pets which included deer, lizards, turtles and frogs. Also he had a sarus crane which became his inseparable companion when he played in the compound surrounding their home.

At the age of eight Geoffrey came to England to attend preparatory school while his family remained in India. His artistic ability was soon recognised at school and he was awarded three honours certificates from the Royal Drawing Society. He went on to the Boys' Grammar School at Ashby-de-la-Zouch, in Leicestershire, and while there won the Chairman's prize of the Royal Drawing Society and also the Society's Gold Star. On the natural history side of his life, he set up a small zoo which contained snakes, lizards, hedgehogs and rats, and his interest in

wildlife continued to grow in spite of being bitten by an adder.

This interest almost cost Geoffrey his life because after cleaning the wounds of a polecat which had been bitten by a rat he contracted the rare and usually fatal Weil's disease. When in a · semi-conscious state he heard the doctor tell his mother and father that they must consider the possibility that he would die. He made a firm resolve to live and, drawing upon the courage and fortitude which was to reveal itself later in his life, made a complete recovery.

He volunteered for the Royal Air Force as an air-gunner at the outbreak of the second World War although he was only seventeen years old, but became frustrated by waiting for his call-up and so joined the Army. From 1942 he served with the Eighth Army and was attached to General Staff Intelligence as a draughtsman. Travelling with Montgomery's forward HQ in the desert gave him the opportunity to study snakes and he became known in the desert as the Eighth Army's 'snake charmer' after an article appeared in the *Eighth Army News* about his reptilian exploits. Later, he saw action at Caen and Falaise and then through Belgium and Holland to the Rhine. There, awaiting his unit's participation in the Rhine crossing, he was walking between the white tapes that should have indicated the area had been cleared of mines, when he trod on an anti-personnel mine. He lost his left foot and sustained compound fractures to his right leg.

At first, Geoffrey had no idea he had suffered these severe injuries; his first recollection was a feeling of awakening from a dream – the reality of the situation did not occur to him for some moments until he noticed his left foot had gone. Then with the

Geoffrey Kinns makes a particularly difficult exit after photographing bats in a Devonshire cave

same fortitude that he had shown earlier in his life, he knew he was losing blood and it must be stopped. He dragged himself forward along a tank track towards the road. Fortunately, he was seen by a passing Brigadier and his batman who dressed his wounds, and this prompt action saved his life. He was sent to a forward hospital and after three operations and convalescence in England he returned to civilian life.

It was during his convalescence period that an incident occurred that had a significant effect on his later life. A farmer asked him to help with the destruction of a family of badgers, which according to the farmer had been causing much damage. In the darkness a dog appeared at the point where the badgers were expected and it was shot and killed. From that moment onwards Geoffrey decided to forsake forever the gun.

He resumed his studies at the Derby School of Art in 1946 and later at the Royal College of Art. After a period of freelance work he joined the Exhibition Section of the Natural History Museum in 1955, as a Temporary Scientific Assistant, and was later promoted to Senior Scientific Assistant and finally to Scientific Officer.

His first attempts at wildlife photography were made with a Voigtlander folding camera and he was delighted with the results which included close-ups of a pair of badgers. From that moment onwards he was committed to photography, a path he has followed ever since. Much of his spare time is spent visiting and photographing in the Scottish Highlands and the RSPB bird sanctuaries – in particular, near Strontian, Argyllshire, Beinn Eighe, Gairloch in Wester Ross and Skye where he has photographed wild cats, pine martens, otters, deer and golden

Below: Voles from Skomer Island, a nature reserve off the Dyfed coast
Below right: A Grey Squirrel

eagles over the last decade. In 1966 he was awarded the *Animals* magazine silver medal for a photograph of a red deer stag taken in the Scottish Highlands. Although Geoffrey has added cine photography to his repertoire, and has made films of eagles for Scottish Television, still photography remains his primary interest.

Geoffrey has an assortment of cameras and equipment including infra-red beam equipment, flash-guns, trip wires, 35mm and 2¼″ × 2¼″ and 2¼″ × 3¼″ cameras. However, most of his wildlife photographs have been taken with a Hasselblad 500C camera, with 250mm and 500mm telephoto lens, and nearly all his photographs are hand held, exceptions being golden eagles and other birds taken from a hide, using a tripod. Many of the smaller mammals are taken with flash, often in captivity.

In 1977 Geoffrey was given the opportunity to retire early from his work at the Natural History Museum and he accepted it to allow himself more time to acquire even higher quality photographs of Britain's mammals. The majority of his photographic work is used for illustrative purposes in books and magazines, although his main purpose is obtaining material for lectures.

Geoffrey has very strong feelings regarding the conservation of wildlife. He believes that lectures and wild life publications for adults and particularly for children can create a better understanding of the plight of some of our mammals and their habitats and that this better understanding will help to ensure a future for them in the British Isles.

Below: A herd of Sika deer

# Photographer's Acknowledgements

During the compilation of this book I realised my great indebtedness to friends and colleagues for their tolerance, interest and kindness throughout the development of my photography and knowledge of wildlife. It commenced with my old headmaster, Mr T. A. Woodcock at Ashby-de-la-Zouch Grammar School who was sympathetic towards my attempts to establish a small animal hospital and his tolerance when escapes caused some confusion in the classrooms and dormitories. Miss Mona Edwards, M.B.E., B.Sc., who until her retirement was head of the exhibition section of the Natural History Museum at Kensington. It was her encouragement that enabled me to develop my interest in the natural history of British Mammals. The Earl and Countess of Cranbrook for their interest in my work and their many kindnesses. Mr S. Meade and Lady Sophie for their help with the photography of a stoat. Dick Balharry, Chief Warden, Nature Conservancy Council, Scotland, and his wife Adeline, for their help and hospitality during my quests to photograph Golden Eagles in their region. Dr Morton Boyd, director Nature Conservancy Council, Scotland and his colleague Dr Derek Ratcliffe, for their valuable assistance. Edwin and Mary Anne Cross, Hugh and Jena Brown, wardens at the Beinn Eighe National Nature Reserve for their continuing hospitality. Major Eric Hunter and his wife Dr Lennox Hunter for their aid and support to my photography of pine martens. Jim and Tina Rowbottom for their help in locating otter sites. Mr Phillip and Jeane Ware, for their courtesies extended to me during my photographic forays in the Wildlife Park in Norfolk. Mr and Mrs William Kingdom for the facilities granted to me for photographing, in particular, close-ups of the wild cat, and other animals. Donald and Bridget Maskell for their help in locating wildlife habitats. The owners and staff of the Wildlife Park, Kingussie, Inverness-shire, for their active assistance. Mikel Utsi and his wife Dr E. J. Lindgren, whose invaluable aid contributed greatly to my reindeer photography. Harry Thompson and Charles Swan, Ministry of Agriculture, for organising the arrangements for the mink photography. Dr Tony Sutcliffe, Alfred Leutscher, Mrs Joyce Pope and my former colleagues at the Natural History Museum for their many kindnesses and encouragement in my pursuit for knowledge of Britain's wildlife. The staff at Hodder and Stoughton whose expertise has been so important to the production of this book. David Burton, B.Sc., for checking the text and last but not least, the mammals without whose presence and co-operation this book would not have been possible.

*Geoffrey Kinns.*

# Bibliography

BEIRNE, B. P. *The Origin and History of British Fauna* Methuen, 1952

BLACKMORE, M. *Mammals in Britain* Collins, 1948

BOORER, M. *Mammals of the World* Hamlyn, 1970

BOURLIÈRE, F. *The Natural History of Mammals* Harrap, 1955

BURTON, M. *Animals of the British Isles* Warne and Co, 1968

CORBET, G. B. and SOUTHERN, H. N. *The Handbook of British Mammals* Blackwell, 1977

CORBET, G. B. *Finding and Identifying Mammals in Britain* British Museum (Natural History), 1975

CROWCROFT, P. *The Life of the Shrew* Rheinhardt, 1957

EDWARDS, K. C. *The Peak District* Collins, 1962

ELTON, C. *Animal Ecology* Sidgwick and Jackson, 1936

FALKUS, H. *Nature Detective* Gollancz, 1978

GARNIS, H. *The Natural History of Europe* Hamlyn 1967

GODFREY, G. K. *The Life of the Mole* Museum Press, 1960

HANÀK, V. *Mammals* Octopus Books, 1977

HARRISON-MATTHEWS, L. H. *British Mammals* Collins, 1952

HEWER, H. R. *Seals* Collins, 1976

HURREL, H. G. *The Fox* The Sunday Times Publications Ltd., 1962

LAWRENCE, M. J. and BROWN, R. W. *Mammals of Britain, Their Tracks, Trails and Signs* Blandford Press 1973

LEUTSCHER, A. *Tracks and Signs of British Animals* Cleaver-Hume Press, 1960.

MILLER, G. S. *Catalogue of the Mammals of Western Europe* British Museum (National History), 1912

MORRIS, D. *The Mammals* Hodder and Stoughton, 1965

NEAL, E. G. *The Badger* Pelican, 1948

ROOTS, C. *Animal Invaders* David and Charles, 1976

THOMPSON, H. V. and WORDEN, A. N. *The Rabbit* Collins, 1956

VESEY-FITZGERALD, B. *British Bats* Methuen, 1949

YALDEN, D. W. *Feral Wallabies of the Peak District* Journal of Ecology, London, 1971. 165. 513–520.

# Official and Voluntary Organisations concerned with the Protection of Wildlife and the Countryside

Habitat of Polecat and Fox

# Official Organisations

NATURE CONSERVANCY COUNCIL, Great Britain Headquarters.
19–20 Belgrave Square, London, SW1X 8PY

COUNTRYSIDE COMMISSION
John Dower House, Crescent Place, Cheltenham, Gloucestershire, GL50 3RA

COUNTRYSIDE COMMISSION FOR SCOTLAND
Battlebury, Redgorton, Perth, PH1 3EW

FORESTRY COMMISSION, Headquarters
231 Corstorphine Road, Edinburgh, EH12 7AT

WATER SPACE AMENITY COMMISSION
1 Queen Anne's Gate, London, SW1H 9BT

# Voluntary Organisations

BRITISH NATURALISTS' ASSOCIATION
Willowfield, Boyneswood Road, Four Marks, Alton, Hampshire, GU34 5EA

COUNCIL FOR ENVIRONMENTAL CONSERVATION
29–31 Greville Street, London, EC1N 8AX

COUNCIL FOR NATIONAL PARKS
4 Hobart Place, London, SW1W 0HY

COUNCIL FOR THE PROTECTION OF RURAL ENGLAND
4 Hobart Place, London, SW1W 0HY

ASSOCIATION FOR THE PRESERVATION OF RURAL SCOTLAND
20 Falkland Avenue, Newton Mearns, Renfrewshire, G77 5DR

COUNCIL FOR THE PROTECTION OF RURAL WALES
14 Broad Street, Welshpool, Powys, SY21 7SD

FAUNA PRESERVATION SOCIETY
Zoological Society of London, Regent's Park, London, NW1 4RY

FRIENDS OF THE EARTH
8 Poland Street, London, W1V 3DG

NATIONAL TRUST
42 Queen Anne's Gate, London, SW1H 9AS

NATIONAL TRUST FOR SCOTLAND
5 Charlotte Square, Edinburgh, EH2 4DU

NATURE CONSERVATION TRUSTS
Information of membership and addresses of County Secretaries can be obtained
from The Society for the Promotion of Nature Conservation, The Green,
Nettleham, Lincoln, LN2 2NR

SCOTTISH WILDLIFE TRUST
8 Dublin Street, Edinburgh, EH1 3PP

SOCIETY FOR THE PROMOTION OF NATURE CONSERVATION
The Green, Nettleham, Lincoln; LN2 2NR

TREE COUNCIL
35 Belgrave Square, London, SW1X 8QN

WORLD WILDLIFE FUND
Panda House, 29 Greville Street, London, EC1N 8AX

WILDLIFE YOUTH SERVICE OF THE WORLD WILDLIFE FUND
Wildlife, Wallington, Surrey

# Index of English Names

Numbers in bold type refer to photographs

# Index of Latin Names

Numbers in bold type refer to photographs